BOOK NO: 1845337

1845337

OUT OF THE SHADOWS

Help for Men
who Have Been
Sexually Assaulted

Sarah Stott

D1477795

Russell House Publis

First published in 2001 by:
Russell House Publishing Ltd.
4 St. George's House
Uplyme Road
Lyme Regis
Dorset DT7 3LS

Tel: 01297-443948
Fax: 01297-442722
e-mail: help@russellhouse.co.uk

British Library Cataloguing-in-publication Data:
A catalogue record for this book is available from the British Library.

ISBN: 1-898924-98-8

Typeset by The Hallamshire Press Limited, Sheffield
Printed by Creative Print and Design Group

Russell House Publishing

Is a group of social work, probation, education and youth and
community work practitioners and academics working in
collaboration with a professional publishing team. Our aim is to
work closely with the field to produce innovative and valuable
materials to help managers, trainers, practitioners and students. We
are keen to receive feedback on publications and new ideas for
future projects.

CONTENTS

For Paul with love

ACKNOWLEDGEMENTS

I am indebted to a number of people who supported me in writing *Out of the Shadows*. I would like to thank those from Gippsland Centre Against Sexual Assault and Geelong Rape Crisis Centre (in Australia) who took the time to read and comment on earlier drafts. I am also grateful to Chris Dawson, Chris Laming, Max Clarke and Gary Lawler, all of whom provided me with valuable feedback.

Above all, I extend my gratitude to the male survivors who contributed to *Out of the Shadows* whose commitment to helping other male survivors is inspirational. A final thank you to all the male survivors, of all ages, whom I have worked with over the years. They shared their experiences with me with honesty, hope and courage. I hope that *Out of the Shadows* enables many other male survivors to share those qualities and to recognise their own.

Sarah Stott

INTRODUCTION

Out of the Shadows has been written to provide factual information about male children and adults who have been subjected to sexual assault. It aims to help these male survivors understand how sexual assault may have affected them and offers practical suggestions about how to deal with those effects.

Use *Out of the Shadows* in the way that best suits you: read straight through it all in one go or just dip in and chose the most relevant parts.

The first chapter contains individual men's stories of rape. They are placed at the beginning of the book because people will usually read the personal accounts first, even when they are found at the end of a book!

Those involved were willing to share their experiences with a wider audience in order to help and support other male survivors. They wanted to give all male survivors permission to speak out about personal, painful and difficult things. Their stories demonstrate the courage and resilience that all survivors have, and offer hope for recovery.

The stories represent a wide range of experiences. They may or may not match yours: everyone's experience is unique.

Chapter 2 offers information about the sexual assault and rape of male **children**. Learning about sexual assault can empower you and help to break down the secrecy.

Chapter 3 deals similarly with the sexual assault and rape of **adult** males. Examples of men's individual experiences of rape can be found at the end of the chapter.

The fourth chapter concentrates on recovery. It describes how sexual assault affects men and boys and looks at some of the emotions you may have.

Chapter 5 details practical ways of resolving some of the issues and offers information about your legal options.

If you want to tell someone about this book

Please photocopy this page and the order form on p. xi and give it to them.

How to obtain this book

It is the goal of the author to offer help to males who have been sexually assaulted. A central part of this goal is to make *Out of the Shadows* available as easily as possible to people who may not want themselves or other people involved to be identified. Here are details of how to order the book. Please choose the one that you are most comfortable with.

- ## *From bookshops*
  Take a copy of the order form to almost any bookshop and ask them to order it for you. The information they need is on the form. If you do not wish to be identified, ask a friend to do this for you.
  ISBN 1-898924-98-8.

- ## *From Russell House Publishing*
  Read the next paragraph carefully. Then complete the order form and send it to us with your cheque.

If you do not wish to receive any subsequent mail from Russell House Publishing or anyone else, please make sure you tick the relevant box on the order form. But please bear in mind that publishers are human and sometimes make mistakes, like anyone else. If you want an absolute guarantee that your name is kept 100% confidential, ask a good friend to send the order form on your behalf and have them write the cheque for you as well.

✔ Please supply the following items:

———— copies of *Out of the Shadows* (ISBN 1-898924-98-8)

£9.95 each ————

Add postage and packing (UK) £1.50 <u>per item</u> (Elsewhere) £2.50 <u>per item</u>

PAYMENT: Individual customers: please pay in advance.

☐ I enclose a cheque made payable to **Russell House Publishing Ltd.**

☐ Please send an invoice and my purchases to my organisation for payment on receipt.

IN A RUSH? QUESTIONS? Please fax or phone: we will respond by return.

☐ If you do not wish to receive any mail from us or other organisations, please tick this box.

☐ If you wish to receive news of other RHP books, but do not want your name on any mailing list provided to any other organisations, please tick this box.

Name _____ BOOK

Address _____

_____

_____

Postcode ——————————— **Phone number** ———————————

Send orders to: **Russell House Publishing Ltd, 4 St. George's House, The Business Park, Uplyme Road, Lyme Regis, Dorset DT7 3LS**
Phone: 01297-443-948; Fax: 01297-442-722

Chapter 1

MEN'S EXPERIENCES OF SEXUAL ASSAULT

Mark

I can remember my Dad on the footpath the day he was leaving. He gave me and my brother the choice about whether we went with him or stayed with Mum. I chose to go with him but ended up staying with Mum anyway. He didn't want us. I remember terrible arguments and one time he threatened to run a butcher's knife through Mum.

Mum had to go out to work. I remember coming home to an empty house—a horrible feeling in itself. I was nine. The loneliness, I used to cry a lot. I was not much good at school. I didn't have any real friends and I wasn't allowed to have pets. My brother lived with my grandmother. I felt he was favoured by everyone. I was always in trouble.

I remember a time; it was a Saturday afternoon. I was told to stay in the car outside the hotel. Mum and her friends went in for a drink. Being a typical little kid I jumped into the driving seat and pretended to be driving the car. This bloke opened the passenger door and got in. He pointed a knife at me and told me he was going to kill me. I was so scared. He kept changing the knife from one hand to another. Just total fear—I wanted to run but I was too scared to move. There was another man with him who kept trying to coax him to leave me alone and eventually he did. It seemed like an eternity before Mum came back. I couldn't say if they were drunk or not. I told her what had happened but she said 'that didn't happen'. I was horribly confused, so scared and then not being believed by Mum. Not being trusted to tell the truth.

Next door there was a teenager called Barry. He was about 17. He lived with his parents and there were two older boys. He was around during school holidays. He was asked to keep an eye on me after school and during school holidays.

The first time I was at his place he started talking about sex. There was a girl who lived locally about the same age as me who was playing outside. He had his penis out, playing with himself and he started to masturbate me. I wanted to run. He was so much bigger than me. He made me take my pants off and said 'I'm going to fuck you, suck this' and grabbed my head. I went numb, wanting to run, wanting to vomit. It seemed so big. It was the first time I had seen a man's erection. The girl was still playing outside. He raped me then. I was crying, it was so painful. He said 'if you tell anyone I'll kick your fucking head in–I'll tell them what you've done'. I was sore, frightened and confused. I was the one who had done something bad. All this time the girl was outside riding her bike and he kept asking me if I wanted to fuck her.

From then on I tried to avoid him but he seized every opportunity. He threatened me every time. I would say 'No' and he would say 'you want it'. This went on for two years. He always told me I enjoyed it and he would bash me if I would not do it. He said he'd tell people what I had done. I was so frightened that I'd be capable of doing it.

I still find it incomprehensible that an adult man can do that to a child. Feelings of disgust and repulsiveness. I wanted to cry, to be sick. I would cry and he'd tell me to shut up. School holidays— I hated them. You knew it would happen more.

There were cliffs opposite the park and you could climb up them and watch the races on the racecourse. I remember one day climbing up there and he followed me. He got me between the rocks. He said, 'You have to let me fuck you whenever I tell you'.

I wasn't safe anywhere. I remember climbing down from the rocks and I went to my room. I just lay there. Most times I'd cry. I can remember lying there before when my parents argued. I just wanted it to stop. I was always in trouble. I was the target for bullies. Most of the time I lived in fear. The only time I felt safe was when I went to Nan's. You could ride your bike there and not feel afraid. One day at Nan's I did something I shouldn't have. There was a watchdog chained up and no one was supposed to go near him. I did though. He wouldn't hurt me and he wouldn't let anyone else hurt me. The only thing that protected me. I wasn't allowed pets at home.

One time we were in my room, I don't know how he came to be in my room. I remember Barry doing it to me. He made me have oral sex. My brother was there and he had an erection and told me to have oral sex with him. I tried but I couldn't. I was even more afraid than usual. I can't remember if he hit me. He must have gone off with Barry because I remember being in the room alone. He went to Nan's after that and we never spoke of it again. Sex is never something I have discussed with him. We only talk about general things. We are brothers in name only. I lost him— the betrayal. I can't rely on anyone or trust them. I'd always prefer to do things myself. I'm frightened of ridicule if I mess up.

When we moved house the sexual assault stopped. I fell back in school, I was below average. I just marked time. I've had times when I've exploded with anger which always got me into trouble. One time my brother was teasing me and I threw a metal rake which hit him in the face. I got a hiding from Mum and my brother was the saint again.

We moved back to a city and my brother and I were put in a boys home. I was 12. I was constantly frightened that I would be sexually assaulted again. We left the boys home a couple of years later and went to a hostel waiting for a house. My brother got into trouble with the police. I've never had a criminal record but I'm not a saint.

I hit puberty late at 14. I was very confused. I knew what was wrong but not what was right. I was going to a co-ed school, marking time. Sex came up in conversation as it does with boys and girls. I was starting puberty and thinking about sex. I didn't seem to mix well. My social skills with girls were zero and social mixing with boys was only casual. We moved so much I didn't form lasting friendships. Obviously, I kept my distance too.

I knew that if a man touched you it was wrong but I didn't know about women. I had no sex education at all. All I knew was from Barry and I knew that was wrong. I was scared of contact. I'd get sexual feelings but I didn't know why. I did not have anyone to ask.

One day when I was working I was walking home. There was a guy who was a lawyer who used to pay young boys for sex. He gave me a lift and propositioned me. I jumped out the car at the lights. I was scared out of my wits.

My first sexual experience was when I was 18 with a young woman who taught me what I needed to know. I've continued to learn with my wife. I recently realised that I prefer to make love with both of us naked. During the sexual assaults I always had clothing on. I need to ensure that making love is different from the assaults. I've learnt not just to think of my sexual pleasure and to understand that good sex means good for both people.

The sexual assaults have affected my relationship with my wife. It has been hard to separate my feelings about the sexual assaults and my feelings about Vietnam. The rejection and betrayal have felt the same. It drove me into myself and I found it hard to love. I must have appeared to be cold and insensitive. I have struggled to understand myself. My low self-esteem was accentuated by Vietnam. I drank and smoked very heavily. Drink almost ruined my marriage and made me hard on my boys. I desperately wanted them to have a better childhood than I did and I got frustrated when they did not reach their potential. Until you almost lose what you have do you realise something was wrong. I did not know who I could trust enough to talk to. Then Vietnam vets did a session on Post Traumatic Stress and I realised I needed help and sought it. This led me to seek help for the childhood sexual assault. At last I could talk, and be understood, without fear of ridicule, without being put down.

The counsellors have been women and I felt that they were more understanding. I could develop a more confidential relationship with them. Understanding from a good wife has made it all more bearable. I've found people being more open. I can talk about it easier, without shame, degradation and hurt that goes with it. I still get hurt and angry when I hear about children being abused.

I understand myself better now. It's been like coming out of a fog. In the past, I existed without really living. The hurt and anger has always been there. It's still there, but it's more under control, more in perspective. My anger is more directed to the perpetrators. I handle the hurt better. I take responsibility for my own feelings.

I carried it around for 40 years. It gnawed away at me. I am grateful for the help I have got from counsellors. The help was there for the asking. I hope I can help by telling my story to other men. The more I have talked the easier it has become.

Peter

I was one of a large family living on a farm. Our family was that strict and we led a sheltered life, no TV, radio or anything. I was really close to my brother. I was a very hyperactive child. Mum and Dad had a bad marriage and there was a lot of violence. Mum's brother, my uncle, had two sons who were older than us. The cousins used to come to our place for holidays and weekends.

The older cousin was 13 and I was seven. Because he was older he was given responsibility for us younger kids and could take us to lots of places without adult interference. I can't remember exactly when it started. There were so many times he assaulted me. It went on for so long. It just went on and on and on. He told me it was perfectly normal and that he and other boys had done it. He told me that was why I had a penis, for other boys to play with. It happened everywhere, whenever he had an opportunity. He would make me walk around naked and simulate sex with me. He made me have oral sex and attempted anal penetration and would get me to do those things to him.

At the time I believed him when he said it was normal. I did not have any other information about sex. By the time I realised it wasn't I was trapped. One time, the first time he had ejaculated through oral sex I felt so sick and disgusting. My brother and I told him we would tell Mum. He said but you've done it too so you'll get into trouble. I was nine then. He anally penetrated me later and tried to get me to do it to him.

When he got older he got his driving licence and would take me places in his car. I kept trying to say no but he'd say 'just one more time'. Eventually when I was 13 he got a girlfriend and a baby and it didn't happen again. I still see him and he waves at me. I confronted him once and asked him why he did it. He still said it was normal and I had done it too. He's got no guilt about it.

All throughout the years of abuse there was trauma in the family. Mum and Dad split and reconciled. One time Mum left in the middle of the night taking my younger sister and brother and leaving me with Dad. I can remember how that felt. I was so upset. Dad worked all the time and was away most of the time. I couldn't tell Dad because he was absent and distant. I couldn't tell Mum because it was her brother and they were really close.

Ever since I was a child I have hated myself. I've felt guilty, ashamed, disgusted and confused. When I hit my teenage years I was totally uncertain about my sexuality. I was attracted to girls but was so unconfident. I experimented sexually with other boys but it made me feel really ashamed and bad. I felt so confused. I blamed myself totally. I didn't stop it.

I left home at 16. I was kicked out of school because I was always in trouble. I picked on other kids, I was a bully. I could never concentrate. I was quite capable but I never achieved anything at school.

When I was 17 I told my Mum about the sexual assault. I wanted to protect my younger siblings. Mum said she believed me and stopped him seeing the younger boys.

I told Dad when I was 19. His first reaction was that I must have enjoyed it and why didn't I tell him. I was so angry and was crying. I was a sobbing mess, I punched the tree and wanted to hit him. His view was that you should control your emotions.

After I left home I became suicidal. I got a rope but a friend took it off me, and then I was going to walk into the sea and never come back. The police chased me, and took me to a psychiatric hospital. I told staff there about the sexual assault. I met my partner when I was 18. We were friends for three months and then began a relationship.

When she became pregnant I was really happy. Towards the end of the pregnancy I started getting really upset. I was cutting my arms with razor blades and smashing myself against fences. I was so angry and the physical pain relieved the anger. I was diagnosed with depression and anxiety. I went downhill and became suicidal. I was so ashamed, guilty and dirty. I felt I was nothing. I felt guilty for everything and felt I had no future. It was the worst time of my life. I can't remember the first 18 months of my son's life. I hacked at myself with razors. I came close to hanging myself a few times. I got hold of my father's gun but he'd taken the bolt out. I'd run off into the fields and go missing. My Dad would come and find me. I felt guilty about everything and anything. I was on heaps of medication and was out of it a lot of the time. I had five admissions to hospital. At one stage I was on nine different medications and I got a toxic reaction and ended up in intensive care. They thought I was going to die. After I came out of hospital I went to a few counselling sessions. My depression was all about the guilt and the shame and bad feelings and belief I'd done something wrong.

I got off most of the medication myself after that. I've seen lots of psychiatrists but only one helped me. I began to get better and then I felt ready for counselling again. I began to make sense of what happened to me. I used to really hate myself but in the last six months I've begun to realise that I'm not a bad bloke. I can be doing good things with my kids and think I'm not doing anything wrong.

I never used to be able to work because I couldn't concentrate and I felt so isolated and alone. I can work now and I'm more in control of my life. I no longer feel hopeless and I can cope when things go wrong. I can make decisions which I never could before. I don't feel the abuser has that power over me any more. I'm in control and I can decide whether to make a statement against him. I don't get so angry at myself so much. I used to punch inanimate objects just to release the anger.

I was so scared that I might be an offender. I was scared to wash my kids in the bath. I was so scared of being a parent. I don't think that now. All that fear and guilt and shame was held inside and it turns into anger which self destructs. If you let out the feelings and release the tears you can get rid of the anger. Everything has really come good.

I've worked out all the shame and blame and guilt with my counsellors and I'm going to go to a group for male survivors.

Andrew

I used to be an outward looking child. I had friends before it happened. I had a younger brother, and an older sister who died before I was born. I always felt that I was 'second choice' for my parents after my sister died. She died eight years before I was born.

What if my sister had lived and she had been the one who was assaulted. You wouldn't wish it on anyone would you? My parents probably took better care of my younger brother after it happened.

I was between six and seven when it happened and it went on for about three weeks. The person who sexually assaulted me had learning difficulties . It was his own personal aberration. He used to meet me off the school bus and take me to this field. People were passing nearby when it happened. He made me play with his penis with a rough leaf. That gave him his kicks. He said he would kill me if I didn't do it or if I told. I believed him. I thought he was going to kill me. I was so scared.

My parents knew something was wrong. I went quiet. They kept at me but then I said I couldn't tell because he'd kill me and then they got the police in. I must have told them. I think he was charged. He must have known it was wrong because otherwise he would not have threatened me. He should have some punishment but something is wrong, it's an illness. They need help as well.

I still felt scared that he'd kill me. I was always looking for him. I had to be careful all the time. I felt I had to be careful and I became too careful, always cautious. I never made friends after that.

I became a loner, riding my bike for hours, staying away from home. I had nightmares and wet the bed until my late teens. I got involved in petty crime and developed a real problem with aggression. I never made any friends. I've found friendships too hard. I was uncommunicative and I think people pick that up and know it's inside you. My childhood was stolen from me so I stole what I missed out on. I won't steal now, I can't have anything that belongs to others.

I went to a secondary modern school but I was probably better at language, reading, words. I didn't do really well. You get used to being discouraged. I've been discouraged all my life. I've been around and had lots of jobs, factory, warehousing, truck assembly. The longest I was in a job was for six years. I've lost most of my jobs because of my aggression and fights. The anger builds up and then I snap. I can't remember what I do when I lose it. I know I could kill someone. I let people get to me. When I get angry I shake afterwards, it's like a release of emotion. One time I stopped myself hitting a male nurse when I was in hospital. I went outside and cried for an hour.

I've seen loads of psychologists and psychiatrists for depression, aggression and suicide attempts. I've been on medication and I've tried lots of different churches over the years. I used to drink heavily but it made me more aggressive so I don't drink any more. I never told anyone about the sexual assault until I told a counsellor last year. She's the only one who broke through. I kept it inside for 46 years.

My relationships with women were non-existent. It was hard because I was frightened. I felt I was not worthy to be with women. I had such low self-esteem and no confidence. I felt totally inadequate in relationships.

I've had one long relationship which started when I was in my late thirties. We were together for eight years. She died of cancer. It ripped me apart, sent me over the edge. It was a really good relationship and I was lucky to have it. I didn't understand sexual relationships before. It's a legacy of the sexual assault that I would never have sex without consent. I would never coerce or try and influence someone to have sex. It must be something loving and pleasurable for both people. I don't want sex, I want to make love.

Disclosing last year to my counsellor was like an explosion. It was just an incredible release, like taking out a cork of a bottle of tears. Trauma just builds inside you over the years. The counsellor understood sexual assault and she knew where I was coming from. It makes a difference to talk to a counsellor who understands what it is about. You can't relate everything that happens in your life to being sexually assaulted but your personality, attitude, character and the general make up of you as a person is based on your child sexual assault experiences. It is the foundation of how you think because you feel it is your fault, you feel ashamed, you feel inadequate. It creates a depth of degradation in your mind.

The trauma never goes away. I can feel it in others. It hurts, constant pain. It stops you achieving and advancing. Once you recognise it you can get some control and overcome it. I've recognised that the power of the abuser ruled my life. I'm beginning to break away from that power. My life is changing for the better. I have a friend and I'm better at controlling my anger. I've made a really close friend. Now I feel I can improve my life rather than make it worse. I want that for other survivors. It is hard to talk but it is the only way to release it and only then can people understand what goes on inside you. If you are having trouble keeping your emotions intact, talk to a professional or a friend before you hurt yourself or others. I did that and now I no longer want to take my own life, I want to live it.

Craig

I must have been about 11 when it started. I used to go to the neighbours' house a lot after school and at weekends. She was really nice to me and used to give me special things to eat and talk to me. Sometimes I'd help her around the house and do the lawns and things like that. I was an only child and I didn't have many friends my age locally. Mum and Dad had their own business and worked really hard. Mum encouraged me to go to the neighbours because she knew where I was and thought I was safe.

She had this amazing collection of soldiers that had been her fathers. They were the old lead ones and I loved playing with them. Looking back I realise I was so innocent. I had no idea what was happening. I hadn't developed any interest in girls and used to keep away from the boys at school who talked about sex.

I can't remember how it started but it progressed from cuddles and stuff. She began to stroke my penis and put it in her mouth. It felt really nice. Then I began to stroke her breasts and eventually perform oral sex on her. At times I felt uncomfortable because I knew it wasn't right and I was confused because it felt good. She told me not to tell because other people would not understand. She told me it was a special gift and I'd learn how to make love to girls.

I became even more withdrawn and was really scared that someone would find out. I started to feel really dirty because I knew it was my fault. I let her do it and I kept going back to do it again. It was exciting and disgusting. I couldn't stop myself and I just felt more and more ashamed. That's when I began to wash myself compulsively. I'd be washing my hands hundreds of times a day.

As I reached puberty I began to understand more and we were having full sex by then. She'd always tell me how lucky I was and not many boys got this sort of thing. That made me feel more freakish and ashamed. I wanted to tell someone but I couldn't risk it.

It stopped when I was 13 because she got a boyfriend who moved in with her. I was relieved and confused. I felt rejected but also freed. Like someone who's done a long jail time but can't cope when they come out. The washing got worse and my parents took me to child psychologists. I couldn't stop it because it was the only thing I could do that made me feel normal, if only for a few seconds.

I've had lots of treatments over the years but they haven't helped. I never told anyone about what happened. I never saw it as abuse. I never connected sexual assault with what happened to me yet I could never tell.

I've had a so called 'normal life'. I'm married with kids. Most of the time the hand washing is ok but it got much worse again last year when my son turned 11. I started to think about it all again and became totally obsessed with cleanliness, my own and my families.

Last year I heard something on the radio when I was driving. They were talking about male sexual assault and female abusers. I was so shocked because I had never considered it and I had always thought it could not have happened to anyone else. I did lots of thinking and eventually told my wife. It was hard for her because she thought it was a kind of young boy 'got lucky' thing but I went to a counsellor and we both began to understand it better. It's been really painful and I still sometimes feel that I was responsible. But it's getting better and I don't have to wash my hands quite so often. I just wish it hadn't taken so long. I wish there was more information around. When no one talks about female abusers it makes their victims feel even more alone.

Matthew

I can't remember it ever not happening. My earliest memories are sexual abuse by my father. It feels like there was nothing else in my life but abuse. I was the first child and only son. My father was a clergyman and seemed to be home a lot more than other kid's fathers. My mother was a teacher. I have two younger sisters. I never told anyone until it came out that he had abused my nephew when I was 40. I still can't tell everything, it's too much to say.

The first clear memory I have is my father ejaculating in my mouth. We were in his shed. I think that was the first time he did that and that's why I remember, but I know the feeling was familiar so I think other things had happened before. I must have been about four. I hadn't started school and my sister was a baby. I thought I was going to die, I couldn't breathe. I couldn't understand why he was doing it.

All my memories of my childhood are defined by the abuse. I remember things happening in every room. Every holiday or special event is marked by a memory of abuse. I know other things happened but I just don't feel them, I only feel the abuse. It was central to my life. I can't remember knowing it was wrong but I knew it was secret. Everything I did was designed to protect the secret. He told me it was a boy thing and that Mum and the girls wouldn't understand. He never had to threaten me or anything. I adored him and would have done anything to please him.

The sexual aspect of the abuse developed over the years and I was very involved in it. The only pain I remember is the first anal penetration. I became highly sexualised and a sort of mutual partner. It was very intense sexually. I never felt attracted to other

17

men and dad and I used pornography a lot. I knew he still had a
sexual relationship with my mother.

I don't know if my mother ever knew. Sometimes I think she must
have but then I know how clever he was, how good at deceiving
he was. I never really had a close relationship with her. I was cut
off from her by the secret. He was all important and we all just
revolved around him. In other ways he was a good father. He
taught me about the world and fishing and nature, all the things
that I love now.

I always felt different from other children at school and I dealt
with this by working hard and achieving academic success. That
protected me somehow. I think I knew I mustn't draw attention
to myself in any way so I concentrated on being normal and
keeping myself to myself. It's almost as if I didn't need anyone
else.

It continued until I was 19. Although by then I knew it was wrong
it still felt normal. It was when I started a relationship with a
woman that I became depressed. I was very ill for years but I never
told anyone. I have always held back in my relationships,
emotionally and physically. I find it hard to ejaculate during
intercourse and I don't ever feel close to anyone. I feel like I'm
still keeping the secret although it's not a secret any more. I have
avoided having children. I fear I would abuse them so its safer
not to.

When my sisters' children told about what their grandfather was
doing it was a huge crisis for me. I never imagined he would do
it to others because I had always assumed responsibility for what
happened. I could see how young and vulnerable they were but
I couldn't see myself as ever being that vulnerable. I told my sisters

eventually after my father was charged. I couldn't tell the police. Thankfully, my mother had died by then and never had to know.

I still see him and feel responsible for him. I think I always will.

I am a fragmented person. There is the man who the world sees and the real me who I can't show anyone. It's like my real self was formed around the abuse. I am making progress though it feels very slow. It helps to know that I'm not the only one struggling with these things.

Chapter 2

UNDERSTANDING CHILD SEXUAL ASSAULT

Most children who experience sexual assault will find a way to make sense of it in a way that blames themselves. This is because children do not have the knowledge or the skills to understand why it happened. As a result, survivors may grow to adulthood believing, thinking and feeling certain things about themselves and their experiences which may, in fact, be based on false information. The starting point for resolving the difficulties sexual assault can cause is correct information about sexual assault and the impact it has on children. This information can also be helpful for those people who are trying to support you.

This chapter offers general information about child sexual assault, perpetrators and the impacts sexual assault can have.

What is Child Sexual Assault

Child sexual assault covers a range of experiences which involve sexual activity perpetrated on a child by an adult or more powerful person. The perpetrator is likely to have a relationship with the child that involves either an emotional or an actual authority over the child.

Sexual assault involves some form of sexual contact which can include the following:

- Contact between genitals, anus, mouths, fingers, objects. It includes sexual activity the victim is forced to perform on the perpetrator or another victim.
- Being exposed to sexual activity.
- Inappropriate, or 'inadvertent' touching.
- Watching, or invasion of privacy.

- Exposure to pornographic material, videos and magazines.
- Taking photographs/videos of the victim.

Sexual assault is sexually, physically and emotionally abusive. It breaches the personal boundaries all human beings are entitled to. Sexual assault is always criminal.

Sexual assault may feel terrifying and painful to a child but it may also not always feel abusive, although it is usually confusing. It may be exciting, pleasurable or comforting for the child and many offenders will make sure that it does not feel abusive in order to keep the child silent. Even if the experience does not feel abusive for a child it does not mean that it is not exploitative and criminal.

Male survivors sometimes have difficulty recognising they have been sexually assaulted for a number of reasons:

- If the assaults did not involve fear or pain, boys and men are likely to see themselves as responsible and will not recognise it as abusive.
- If the perpetrator is female it is difficult for male survivors to classify the experience as assault when our culture tells boys that sex with older women is educational.
- If the assaults involved sexual arousal, or the victim did not fight back, most survivors will believe it was their fault and therefore not see it as abuse.
- It is hard for males to admit to being a 'victim' because to do so may indicate weakness or homosexuality.

Child sexual assault can be categorised by *who* the offender is:

- Sexual assault by a family member (incest) who may live with the victim or have close contact with them. There is an existing relationship with a child and the perpetrator is likely to be trusted by the child and the adults around them. The relationship between the child and the perpetrator may be a close and loving one and the abuse creates confusion, shame and emotional turmoil for the child. The child may be made to feel special or needed by the perpetrator. The child may be silenced by overt or covert threats to the child, other family members or pets, and will assume responsibility for the secret and the consequences of telling. Incestuous assaults may continue for many years and span more than one generation.

- Sexual assault by an adult connected to the family or the community who creates a level of trust between the child and the family and often offer positive relationships for the child and the adults. These offenders can spend some time building up relationships with the express purpose of achieving an opportunity to sexually assault the child and ensure the child's silence.

- Sexual assault by an adult with authority e.g. clergy, teachers, doctors, whose position in society gives them automatic trust and unquestioned power over a child. Disclosure is extremely difficult as the offender's position offers them protection even if the child does tell.

- Sexual assault by an older child, usually an adolescent who uses available opportunities when they occur e.g. babysitting.

- Sexual assault by another child, called 'peer' sexual assault where children perpetrate sexual activity with other children which is outside the realm of normal 'sex play'. 'Normal' sex play involves mutual curiosity and will not involve force or coercion.

- Sexual assault by a stranger which usually occurs in a public place. These are rare compared with assaults by people known to the child.

Perpetrators have two primary aims, to create the opportunity to sexually assault the child and to ensure the child's compliance and silence. They may achieve this through force, threats and injury. They may be sadistic and ritualistic in their assaults, they can act alone or with others. Some offenders are active participants in paedophile rings.

Other offenders use bribes, blackmail and threats to ensure a child's co-operation and silence. Offenders will often use a 'grooming' process which desensitises the child to touch and semi-sexual play, e.g. play fighting, tickling and creates a warm relationship. The child becomes uncertain about the nature of sexual contact and confused about affection, approval and attention.

Sexual assault can happen to any child, at any time, in any circumstance. Children are essentially vulnerable just by being children. It is impossible for children to protect themselves against a perpetrator intent on sexually assaulting them. Class, gender, race, religion, age, disability do not protect children, and survivors come from all walks of life and all kinds of families.

There are gender differences in the sexual assault of children which are related to the different experiences in society for boys and girls. Historically, the understanding of child sexual assault has focused on girls because the research showed that girls were at greater risk. However, it is now emerging that the child sexual assault of boys has been underestimated because of the societal taboos that prevent males admitting to being a victim. Generally speaking, the fear of being identified as gay, the fear of being seen as weak, and the difficulty in recognising abuse has contributed to the sexual assault of boys being underestimated. This has steadily been changing over the last decade and attention is being given to the experiences of boys and men. Girls remain at greater risk of sexual assault but this does not mean that boys are lesser victims.

Statistics for the sexual assault of boys are unclear because it has been hard for boys and men to disclose. This is beginning to change for boys, at least, and estimates suggest that one in five boys (Mathews, 1996) will experience some form of sexual assault before they turn 18. It is always difficult to get an accurate picture of how common sexual assault is because of the secret and shameful nature of the crime. The most available statistics are from the police and sexual assault counselling services. It is believed that only 10 per cent of all sex offences are reported to police. Some sexual assault counselling services report a third of their service users are male.

Research shows that boys are more likely than girls to be assaulted outside the family (Mathews, 1996). It is common to hear parents say they did not warn their sons in the same way as they warned their daughters about sexual assault. Girls appear to be at greater risk within their families. Age is also a factor, with younger boys being assaulted by family members and boys over ten being more at risk from perpetrators outside the family (Briggs, 1995)

Boys do not receive the same sex education as girls and are less well informed about how their bodies work. Teenage magazines available for girls have information which is not available to boys in the same way (Briggs, 1995). This can make boys vulnerable to perpetrators who will exploit boys' natural sexual curiosity which exists from an early age and is reinforced by their peer group.

Adolescence is generally a vulnerable time for boys when there is a natural interest in sex which perpetrators will exploit, enticing adolescents with alcohol, pornography, cigarettes, money or drugs which effectively prevents the victim from disclosing for fear of getting into trouble.

Although more boys are coming forward for support there is no doubt there is an enormous number of adult men who are struggling with abusive sexual experiences in childhood who feel unable to access support or to admit that it has happened.

Understanding Perpetrators

Perpetrators include parents, siblings, cousins, grandparents, aunts, uncles, family friends, neighbours, teachers, care workers, clergy, coaches, friends' parents, other children and strangers. They cannot be recognised or identified except by their actions. Perpetrators of child sexual assault are predominantly male and heterosexual and are most likely to start offending in their teens. Their motivation is to abuse children, and gender is often less important than opportunity. Many perpetrators will have 'normal' sexual relationships with adults.

There are differences in their patterns of offending which can be broadly described as:

- Perpetrators who target children related to them, sometimes referred to as intra familial offenders. These offenders can continue to offend for many years against their children, grandchildren, nieces, nephews etc. These include men who may target single mothers to gain access to their children.
- Extra familial perpetrators will target children known to them and can have a preference for boys whom they will access easily through sporting or other 'male' activities. These

perpetrators (sometimes called career paedophiles) can devote their lives to assaulting children and may have hundreds of victims and go undetected forever. They are likely to be in contact with other perpetrators and will use every opportunity they have to sexually assault. Often these perpetrators will also target girls in order to make them have sexual contact with other children, to produce photographs and videos or to procure them for other paedophiles.

- Some adult men (and women) report being assaulted by women. These assaults are usually incestuous or involve a 'seduction' of an adolescent boy. Sometimes this is difficult for victims to recognise as sexual assault because we are taught that men are the sexual aggressors, and so cannot then be the victim of abuse by women. We are also taught that males are always available for sex, so the young teenager who is 'seduced' by an older woman is seen as lucky although the experience may feel confusing. Female perpetrators are in the minority but it does happen and has different challenges for the victims' recovery.

Understanding why perpetrators sexually assault children is a challenge. We would all like to believe child sexual assault is a rare and unlikely occurrence. However, the reality is that there is an epidemic of child sexual assault and when we turn a blind eye we encourage perpetrators by continuing to keep sexual assault secret and hidden. There are no clear cut reasons about why children get sexually assaulted and the reasons are as varied as the perpetrators. There are many levels of explanation.

A popular explanation for sex offenders is that they were victims of child sexual assault themselves. This is not strictly true. Given that approximately a third of the male population has been assaulted as children, there would be phenomenal numbers of offenders around if this were the case. There would also be greater evidence of female perpetrators. Estimates are that about 2 to 5 per cent of the adult male population are child sex offenders or have the potential to be so (Lew, 1988).

A number of offenders do have a history of abuse in childhood but there are far more non offenders with a history of child sexual assault. No one is clear why some victims will become offenders and most will not. There appears to be a closer link between physical abuse and sex offending (Urquiza and Capra, 1990). Victims who experienced prolonged sexual assault in childhood which involved a high level of degradation, pain and terror are most at risk of developing sexual offending patterns (Urquiza and Capra, 1990).

Other explanations for perpetrators depend on personal inadequacies, in particular, a difficulty in making relationships. Offenders appear to have a distinct need for power over others and children are the easiest group to establish power over. Gratification occurs from being able to make a child do anything they want. 'How can I get to be alone with the children so that if I want to go to the zoo, we'd go to the zoo, if I want to stay home, we stay home, if I want to go skinny dipping, we'd go skinny dipping, if I want to rape them, I rape them' (O'Connor and Petrakis, 1999).

Some offenders gain emotional gratification from the perceived love and closeness they develop with their victims especially when they can condition/train the child to initiate sexual activity.

Often people try to make sense of perpetrators by believing that they must be 'sick'. The reality of sexual assault is so abhorrent that the only way to make sense of it is to believe that the offender is mentally ill. This is not the case. Sexual offenders have no greater incidence of mental illness than the general population.

Perhaps the only truly valid explanation is that perpetrators enjoy assaulting children. It meets their physical and emotional needs. They like it, it is compulsive and they get away with it because our society allows children to be abused. Children are essentially powerless compared to adults, physically, verbally, emotionally, mentally. Children are seen as possessions, reflections of adults, to be controlled and monitored but somehow less emotionally vulnerable. Their feelings are seen as less valid than an adult's, for example, adults often fall into the trap of thinking children do not understand and therefore, do not feel, or if they do, they will forget. The opposite is actually true. If children have less knowledge, they are less able to make sense of the trauma which increases the emotional impact and compounds the effects. Even if children forget a trauma they remember the feelings associated with it.

The Impacts

The effects of sexual assault are both short and long term. There are immediate impacts as a result of abuse and there are long term difficulties. Many factors influence how people cope with being assaulted e.g. personality, support, reactions to disclosure, the nature of the assault and the relationship with the offender. How boys and men cope with sexual assault is closely linked to how males are taught to behave, feel and think.

Initially, there is the impact of the actual experience of assault. If it involves force, coercion, violence, a child may believe that they will die. If the abuse involves warmth and affection the child is trapped by the fear of disclosure. If the abuse involves fun and excitement the child is silenced by their belief that it is their fault. If the abuse involves a family member, the child is caught in the net of family relationships and the consequences of telling.

During repeated and ongoing sexual assault a child has to find a way to accommodate what is happening to them. This can be understood by seeing the child as a hostage when, in order to survive they must please their captor. Children may have to live their entire childhood under this threat.

Sexual assault leads to numerous feelings that the child has to deal with. The following is not an exhaustive list of what a child has to cope with if they are sexually assaulted but a broad outline of some of the difficulties they may face:

- There is constant fear of being found out, fear of threats being carried out, fear of what happens if they tell.
- There is confusion about the perpetrator if he is loved and trusted, confusion about the sexual assault itself and the child's reactions to it.
- A child may feel isolated, different, alone and unable to share the secret.
- Often children will experience severe anger having outbursts of rage which inevitably get them into trouble.
- Children will feel guilty and responsible for the assaults which is increased if other children are involved.
- Sexual arousal is normal during sexual assault and confirms the child's belief that they are responsible and entrenches their self hatred.
- A child's normal physical, emotional, sexual, and educational development is interrupted, often with long term consequences.

- If the child discloses, there is likely to be disruption to family relationships even if the offender is outside the family.

- There is the ongoing struggle to make sense of what is happening. A child is likely to blame themselves, believe they are dirty and damaged. They may develop a sense of themselves as bad.

- Boys may fear they are gay because of the assault and because from an early age most children are exposed to the beliefs that it is unacceptable to be gay. Any primary school playground confirms what a strongly homophobic society we live in. For boys who may be gay this adds an extraordinary pressure on them, leading to intense turmoil and a greater risk of suicide in adolescence.

- Boys may fear that they will become an offender. The idea that sexual assault creates perpetrators is strongly held and most boys are aware of this. This is yet another secret burden for male survivors who fear that if they disclose, they are automatically branded as a perpetrator.

- Children carry the terrible dilemma of keeping the secret or coping with the consequences of disclosure.

- There is a fundamental loss of innocence and trust in the world. Children lose any sense of safety which is essential for all children to grow and develop.

- Children's sexuality becomes distorted. Their sexual knowledge comes from the abuse and can define their own sexuality. They can lose any sense of control over their bodies and can begin to emotionally separate from their physical being. Children can be confused about the abuse and the sensations they get, as well as being confused about sex and love.

Under these traumatic circumstances a child tries to create ways of dealing with their pain. Some of these ways are essentially self destructive and can set up patterns in adult life, but remain the only way a child can find of bearing the unbearable feelings. Some of the behaviours you might expect in children in these circumstances are sleeping problems, nightmares, angry outbursts, wetting and soiling, self mutilation, overt masturbation, repeating the abuse. In adolescents you may see the same things, as well as substance abuse, extreme risk taking, suicide attempts, sexual acting out. These behaviours serve to express some of the feelings the child has of isolation, depression, anger, guilt and fear.

How feelings are expressed is very much related to how children are taught to behave. From very early on boys get the clear message that they must not show when they are physically or emotionally hurt. These attitudes are sexist to both men and women and deny boys and men any avenue for emotional outlet.

Part of the challenge that exists for men recovering from sexual assault is giving themselves permission to feel, and to express their pain.

Chapter 3

UNDERSTANDING ADULT MALE RAPE AND SEXUAL ASSAULT

This chapter has been written for men who have experienced rape/sexual assault as an adult. It is designed to help you understand what has happened to you and to reassure you that you are not alone. Ideas about recovering from the trauma that sexual assault causes are in the following chapter about recovery.

Male Rape and Sexual Assault

The recognition of the sexual assault of males has steadily been increasing since the mid 1980s, with a gradual acknowledgement of the impact it has on men's lives. However, the focus of this attention has mainly been on the childhood sexual assault of males with little emphasis on the experiences of adolescent and adult males. The reasons for this seem to be that it is more difficult for people to recognise that adult men can be vulnerable either physically or emotionally.

We are all brought up to believe that men are strong and powerful so it is challenging to realise that adult males may be at risk of sexual assault in broader society as well as in prisons or the gay community. This kind of thinking protects us from the frightening reality that adolescent boys and men are at risk.

Sexual assault of men has always existed and is always an expression of the power an individual or a group has over others. It is used to humiliate and undermine the victim's masculinity and sense of self. In wars, rape is seen both as a reward for the 'winners' and as punishment for the 'losers', when not only are males raped by the 'winners', but the women and children (who are seen as 'belonging' to the 'losers') are raped as a further humiliation to those who have been overcome. Sexual assault becomes a clear illustration of the power of the rapist and the vulnerability of the victim. In Greek mythology there are many stories of men being abducted for the purpose of rape. In Roman times men were raped as punishment for adultery. During the First World War the Turks raped their prisoners to increase their humiliation. The most famous example of this was Lawrence of Arabia who suffered greatly as a result of being raped. Sexual assault is used to punish, humiliate and undermine masculinity. It is no wonder that it remains such a hidden crime.

It is difficult for us to know how widespread adult male sexual assault is because of the very real difficulties men have in identifying themselves as victims. The two main difficulties are a fear of being seen as gay and fear of being seen as weak, both of which challenge stereotypes of what men should be. Men tend to only disclose rape when they require medical help for rape injuries or when they access help for other issues. Up until recently in the western world data about male sexual assault was not even collected. This is beginning to change and the figures that are emerging indicate that between 14 and 33 per cent of men have experienced sexual assault (see *The Invisible Boy*, Mathews, 1996). These figures do not include rapes that occur in prisons. Some estimates suggest that 80,000 men are raped every day in prison in the USA (see *Rape of Males*, Donaldson, 1990).

Facts about Male Rape

Sexual assault is a taboo subject in our society and as a result, we all hold certain ideas about how, and why it happens, that sometimes are not true. This section aims to look at the facts and challenge some of the myths that are widely believed about male rape.

Society is able to recognise that male rape occurs within the gay and prison communities but only because most men are not in these categories and therefore male rape is not seen as mainstream. Some people may understand male rape in the prison or gay context because these settings do not include women. The reality is that male rape occurs in all settings and all men are potentially victims. Men are raped by people in authority, by acquaintances and by strangers. The majority of perpetrators are male but women can be involved in raping men as accomplices or in groups. Men are also sexually assaulted in ways that people do not always label as sexual assault e.g. initiation rites and 'pranks' in institutions and workplaces.

Many people find it hard to understand that men can be raped or forced into sexual contact without consent. Society demands that men are always strong and able to defend themselves. Many victims say that prior to the rape they would have died rather than be raped. But the reality is that faced with the threat of injury and death human beings tend to submit because the desire to live is so strong. No one can accurately predict how you will respond in terrifying situations.

Most rapes occur with a significant difference in power between the victim and the perpetrator who may have the advantage of greater strength or numbers, weapons, the element of surprise and intention. There are power differentials between all people based on physical stature, appearance, status, wealth, race, disability, religion, sexuality. Victims can be vulnerable for a number of reasons and perpetrators can be more powerful, for example because they were stronger, there was more than one, they were less intoxicated, or there was an element of surprise, they used violence or weapons or they are a trusted authority figure.

Power and sex are closely linked in our society for men, and sex can be a way of confirming one's own personal power. Bill Clinton, Mike Tyson and Rupert Murdoch are all men who have power (of different sorts) in society and are also seen, by others, to have sexual power and see themselves as sexually powerful. Power gives a sexual licence. Rape is an expression of power in a sexual way. Sex is also one of the few acceptable ways men have of expressing themselves emotionally so sex can become a vehicle for many feelings including anger, fear, hatred, vulnerability, grief and loss. Some men may therefore use sexual ways of resolving deep emotional issues which may result in sexual assault. Other myths exist (and are strongly believed by both sexes) about men being unable to control their sexual urges and therefore have no responsibility for their sexual actions.

To have been raped represents a loss of masculinity or a lack of masculinity in the first place. This fits the myths about gayness being unmasculine and 'weakness' being feminine. The reality is that anyone can be sexually assaulted and perpetrators will use seduction, entrapment, intimidation, threats, coercion and force to enable them to sexually assault. None of these involve consent on the part of the victim.

There are myths about what constitutes male sexual assault. There are common 'pranks' in male environments like shaving pubic hair, putting bicycle pumps in the anus, putting tar or grease on testicles. These activities, that are not always recognised as sexual assault by either the victims or the perpetrators, are allowed and used as a way of making sure people know their place. They are often a feature of initiation in organisations like the armed forces, sport clubs, workplaces etc., and aim to subordinate people e.g. apprentices or new recruits. These practices are commonplace and usually common knowledge. The victims may be severely

40

traumatised but unable to tell anyone of their reactions. In fact the trauma they experience may well be linked to the sexual nature of the violence inflicted upon them. If they do complain they are inevitably seen as weak. Boarding schools, children's homes and other institutions are other examples of places where sexual violence is regularly used, often with the approval of superiors, in order to keep people in their place. Victims are usually powerless to tell or to change things.

The greatest myth about male sexual assault is that the perpetrators are gay. Most rapists are heterosexual or would define themselves as such. One study of male rapists found only 7 per cent were gay (Groth and Wolbert-Burgess, 1980). The majority of male rape happens between heterosexual rapists and heterosexual victims. Heterosexual rape of gay men occurs as a form of gay bashing and punishment. Gay rape is more likely to happen in gay relationships or between gay acquaintances. Adolescents, who see themselves as heterosexual, may be targeted by a homosexual rapist who is likely to have multiple victims. While gay men are raped, they are not more vulnerable than the general population. While we believe that rape is a predominantly gay activity it confirms victims' fear of their sexuality having been taken away or having been made gay by the assault. Victims hold the damaging belief that something 'gay' about them caused the rapist to do it. Sexual assault and sexual orientation are *not* connected.

Rape in the gay community is no different to that in the heterosexual community, except that gay men may be even less likely to report because they do not wish to confirm a negative view of their community. There is date/acquaintance rape, rape within relationships and a smaller proportion of stranger rapes. The impact is no less. Some people believe that gay men would be less affected than straight men because they are 'used to it'. This is the same as saying a prostitute is less affected or a virgin is more affected. Sexual contact without consent is traumatic regardless of who you are or who does it to you.

Men who are raped and sexually assaulted will frequently have erections and ejaculate. This confirms the shame, humiliation and guilt about the assault. Perpetrators will often force the victim to ejaculate as confirmation of their power and ability to humiliate. It needs to be understood that a physical reaction to the assault does not mean either, that you were consenting or that you enjoyed it. Erections and ejaculation can occur for many reasons other than sexual arousal. Fear can produce an erection and pressure on the prostrate gland through anal penetration can cause ejaculation. The fight or flight physical response during terror leads to an adrenaline rush which causes the blood in the body to pump more quickly to the muscles. Be reassured that it is a common reaction in sexual assault and does not mean that you consented.

There is also a myth that sexual assault is less traumatic for men which is linked to those myths about men being less emotional. There is a 'get over it mentality' that finds men's pain difficult to comprehend. This mentality is clear in society's attitudes to men returning from wars where 'heroism' is celebrated but war trauma is ignored and hidden. Men are disenfranchised when it comes to emotion .

Rape in Prison

Rape in prisons and other areas that are confined e.g. psychiatric or military institutions is commonplace. Rape in prison is a clear expression of power, with individuals often having to submit to providing sex for one person in order to gain protection from multiple rape.

Rape in prison has a function. It is a message to men to conform. If you go to prison, rape, or the threat of rape, is part of your punishment. The threat of prison rape is actively used as a deterrent to offenders.

Rape in prison is about power and oppression. In prison there is no power according to income or professional status. Power is linked to group, alliances, colour, strength, appearance. Victims are most likely to be young, first timers, imprisoned for non violent offences. The rapes are likely to be violent, continual and involve multiple rapists.

Prison rape differs from rape in the community because there is no reporting, no prosecution and no sanctions. There are no statistics available, no information and therefore no means of addressing the problem. Rape is useful to prison authorities to keep control because it allows inmates to find their own power structure. There is no access to counselling or support for prison rape victims. Prison rape victims are effectively silenced. An Australian study carried out by Dr Heilpern (1997) in nine prisons found a quarter of all prisoners between 18 to 25 had been raped.

The effects of rape for prisoners are brutalising. Many victims are imprisoned for drug offences and may well have been previous victims of childhood sexual assault or rape. The fact that victims cannot disclose or access support increases the impact.

Rape Trauma Syndrome

Rape Trauma Syndrome is the name for the set of symptoms that rape survivors are likely to experience. The first stage involves denial and disbelief which can lead to 'blocking out' the memories of the assault. Guilt, shame and a sense of humiliation are central for the victim as well as a real sense of stigma, believing oneself to be different, and inferior. Blaming oneself, anxiety, confusion and depression are all likely. Survivors may feel vulnerable and powerless and may go to great lengths to protect themselves from this feeling. Other symptoms include sleeping difficulties, nightmares, panic attacks, relationship difficulties, inability to trust, drug, alcohol, eating problems, extreme rage, mood swings, constant fear, inability to relax.

It can be extremely helpful just to recognise that some of your difficulties are related to experiences of sexual violence. This enables you to begin to make sense of how you feel and how you react to those feelings. It is the first step in recovering. The chapter on recovery offers detailed information about emotional reactions and offers ideas about dealing with them.

Mark

I was 16. I had left home because of problems and was living in a hostel with six other men. I got on really well with one of the staff. He was in his twenties. He listened to me and helped me with benefits and stuff. One night I lost my key and had to wake him up to get into the house. He said come into my room and I'll make you a cuppa. I was waiting for him to come back from the kitchen and was looking at his music. I felt a hand over my mouth from behind and the cold blade of a knife against my throat. He marched me over to the bed and said he'd kill me if I made a sound. He bent me over and pulled down my pants and then he raped me. He said I was a dirty fag and he knew I wanted it. He did and said terrible things. When he finished he said if I ever told he'd kill me. I went to my room and put things against the door. I went to bed and stayed there for two days when the police knocked down the door and took me to a psychiatric hospital. I didn't talk for weeks. He'd told them that I'd been acting crazy for months. Everyone believed him. I did not tell anyone until I went to counselling when I was 25. I made a statement to the police ten years later and in the end he went to prison. I've always thought that this made me gay and that was why he picked me. I realise now that I had been attracted to men before the rape and that my sexuality was separate from the assault. But I didn't know that then and it caused me years of hell in my head.

Luke

I was raped when I was 19 years old. It was my first job and I was eager to please my employers. I had all the usual teasing and stuff from the older blokes but nothing nasty. One day, after work, the boss offered me a beer in the office. He was there with another of the older workers. Everyone else had gone home but I had no sense of any danger. I thought he was just being friendly to the new boy. They locked the door and repeatedly raped me orally and anally. I tried to struggle but I was so scared and they were so strong. In the end I just let them do it. It was so awful. I couldn't do anything to stop them. I was so humiliated because they made me ejaculate. I wasn't able to stop myself. I have never forgiven myself. I trust no one. For years I thought they had done some permanent damage to my body. I was too frightened to get close to anyone but I had sex all the time, I kept trying to prove that I was normal. I knew I wasn't gay but I thought anyone would think so if I told them. Then I saw a programme on male rape and I realised that I was not a freak, it did happen to other people. I phoned a helpline then and began to understand that it was not my fault.

Shane

I was raped when I was 29 by two straight men. I'd been in a gay pub with some friends and these guys were waiting outside when we left. My car was parked some distance away and they followed me after I'd said goodnight to my friends. I didn't feel like I was in danger because I'm a big guy and quite fit. When I got to my car they ran up behind me and said they had a gun which they put against my head. I could feel it. I always thought I'd fight back if anyone tried to hurt me but I was so scared I froze. I did everything they told me to do. They said they were punishing me for being gay. They raped me, in various ways humiliated me. Life has never been the same. My relationship broke up, my partner found it hard to believe that I hadn't fought back. I've become a hermit. I never go out and I live in constant fear. I think everyone will think I deserved it because I'm gay.

Chapter 4

RECOVERY

Recovery

This chapter offers information on recovery from sexual assault and describes some of the emotions you may have.

Sexuality is at the core of all human beings. It is part of how we see ourselves and how we relate to others. It is a deeply personal and individual part of our sense of self. Sexual assault can fragment our sense of self and recovery needs to rebuild this. People who experience sexual assault can and do recover, often with greater self-knowledge, strength and confidence than before.

The consequences of sexual assault trauma are many and varied. How people feel after sexual assault is influenced by many factors, including their supports, the reaction of police and the legal system if they report, physical injuries (sexual and non-sexual) and other broader issues such as personality, self esteem, relationships, sexuality, race, religion, culture, disability, prior victimisation, whether they are recovering from adult or child sexual assault.

The feelings that survivors struggle with can manifest themselves in many ways. It is important to recognise that these are behaviours which serve the purpose of making the feelings less painful in one way or another. This can be through denying the feelings, pretending they are less important than they are or just blocking them out altogether.

The feelings are often expressed by people developing personal difficulties. These can be; depression, anxiety, suicidality, poor self-esteem, self-hatred, problems in relationships with men, women and children, employment difficulties, drug and alcohol abuse, eating difficulties, distorted body image, inability to relax or be spontaneous, overachievement, perfectionism, psychiatric problems, obsessive compulsive disorder, violence, including sexual violence towards others, explosive rage, sexual problems, sleep difficulties, nightmares, flashbacks, excessive sexual activity, lack of sexual activity, criminal activity and paranoia.

Some people who have been sexually assaulted lead lives that are unaffected by their experiences. It is not inevitable that survivors will suffer long term problems and some survivors may only struggle from time to time with difficulties.

The first task of recovery is to make the links between thoughts, feelings, behaviours and the experience of sexual assault. Many men will talk about the sexual assault as not having been a problem, or they forgot about it, or they thought it was dealt with, or it was no big deal. It is only when aspects of their life become difficult that they may link it to the sexual assault.

Problems often emerge at crucial life stages, e.g. puberty, consensual sexual activity, becoming a parent. Most feelings and behaviours are attempts to protect oneself from the feelings associated with the assault. Denial, minimising or blocking out may have been essential to survive in childhood. But as an adult, those ways are no longer needed and may get in the way of living.

As you begin to recover you need to distinguish what your emotional reactions are, how they impact on you and how you show them. It can be liberating to try and understand how you feel and find ways of expressing that. Men are disadvantaged in their emotional expression which often gets channelled into other things. Society gives men the message from early childhood that it is unmasculine to express emotion except for anger or through sex. Having permission and opportunity frees men up to talk about the whole range of emotions they experience.

Some of the most common emotional reactions during recovery are discussed below.

Anger

Anger is in many ways a healthy emotion. It is a response to injustice. It is right to feel angry if you are deliberately harmed by others. It can create energy to change things. It can also be dangerous when it leads to violence or is directed towards the wrong people. It can also become obsessive and cause a festering bitterness when it paralyses rather than fuels appropriate energy. Men are given certain messages about anger and are expected to be angry if, for example, their loved ones or their property is threatened. Anger becomes an acceptable emotion for men but fear or sadness are not. Anger can become the 'dustbin' for other emotions and masks fear, powerlessness, hopelessness, grief.

For sexual assault survivors it is often too scary to be angry with the perpetrator, if you are a child or in a powerless situation, so it gets saved up until you are less powerless. The anger tends then to be redirected to safer targets or suppressed until it comes out in other ways. Anger can be directed towards oneself resulting in self-destructive behaviours which can include getting into violent activities. Anger needs to be directed to where it belongs.

I kept getting into fights with other men, at work, at pubs, at football. I got into heaps of trouble, but when I was fighting I did not feel like that terrified little boy waiting for my father to come into my room.

When I got angry I felt safe. I didn't feel helpless or weak. In fact I didn't feel anything. Anger blocked out all the other feelings.

Guilt

Guilt is a universal reaction to trauma of any kind because it protects against helplessness. It is less painful to think you could have, or should have, prevented something than to admit your vulnerability, e.g. 'if only' thoughts, 'what if I had...'

Children believe the world revolves around them and will believe and feel that they are responsible for bad things happening e.g. in the event of death or divorce a child will think it's their fault because they were naughty, or they were angry with a parent. It is the only way to make sense of what has happened. An adolescent will believe a sexual assault was their fault because they took alcohol offered or were curious about sexual activity. Adolescence is a time of risk taking which is a vital part of development. Sexual assault can often be a case of being in the wrong place at the wrong time with the wrong person. It is never the victims fault.

The fundamental question for survivors can be 'Why me?', 'Because you were there and because the perpetrator could' are the only answers. Self-blame can become destructive and prevent a real understanding and acceptance of what has happened. Most survivors will blame themselves because to blame the perpetrator is too painful when it is a loved and trusted person.

Many survivors will also blame themselves for the assault of other children when there have been multiple victims.

> *If I had told earlier she wouldn't have been abused.*
>
> (14 year old boy)

> *I knew it was my fault, if I hadn't wanted to go camping with him it wouldn't have happened.*
>
> (25 year old man)

I should have kicked him.

(8 year old boy)

Boys and men are likely to blame themselves for not fighting back believing they were unmasculine not to have prevented it.

Shame and Humiliation

Shame is an emotion we all try to protect ourselves from. It is intense and affects our whole way of seeing ourselves. Sexual assault is shaming because it is confused with sex, secrecy and privacy. We try and hide shameful things which ensures that children remain silent about assault. Perpetrators actively induce shame as a means of control. They humiliate in order to make the child powerless. Survivors tend to keep the most shameful aspects of assaults hidden. For example, it is rare for a child to tell everything in a police statement. They will only disclose the least shameful facts.

Shame is often related to physical arousal during assault or a belief that they 'allowed it to happen'. It can be related to the involvement of others e.g. being forced to engage in the sexual assault of other children or acting out sexually as a result of the assaults. Shame is also linked to fears about sexuality, weakness and loss of masculinity. Shame is often not real, rather a memory related to the assault and encouraged by the offender. Addressing the shame you feel becomes a way of accepting yourself.

I suddenly realised that I did not need to feel ashamed any more. He was the one who did shameful things to a five year old boy.

I felt ashamed because I thought other people would think I was an abuser. Once I realised that I knew I wasn't, I was able to get rid of that shame.

Sadness

Recognition of the loss and sadness associated with child sexual assault is an essential step to recovery. There is a need to mourn the loss of childhood, innocence, control, trust, opportunities, sexuality, in order to acknowledge what has been done to you. Sadness is difficult for men to express because of the messages men get about being sad. Society is uncomfortable with male grief. Often men say that when they do express sadness or vulnerability, people in their life are uneasy and do not know how to react.

Although it may be difficult to show your grief and sadness it does not mean it is not there and there are many ways of expressing it. Crying is a healthy and natural response to pain, in fact, tears release calming substances in the body. Many men use active types of grieving e.g. physical activity. If you can link these activities with your feelings it can become a positive process rather than a distraction. Some examples are men training for a marathon, creating some furniture or building a garden to honour a lost childhood and mourn the loss of innocence and trust. Other men carry a childhood photo with them or some soft toy which is symbolic of their childhood.

It is often very hard to connect with the child that you were because it means connecting with the pain, but it can also be uplifting to realise that you were a child and unable to protect yourself. Some survivors make this connection when they know a child who is a similar age to them when the assaults started or when they become a father. Only then is it possible to recognise how vulnerable children are. This can then help to reduce the shame and sense of weakness male survivors carry.

My counsellor suggested I went and bought a special teddy bear to carry in my pocket and remind me of myself as a little boy. I thought she was crazy but I found myself in the toy shop looking at the cuddly toys and feeling that I really wanted one. I spent a long time choosing one and I took him everywhere with me. I even put him on my pillow at night and my girlfriend thought that was great. It didn't make me feel pathetic or weak but the opposite really. I felt strong that I could do something positive.

Fear

It is a toss up whether fear or sadness is the most difficult emotion for men to express. Fear has a purpose for everyone—we need to feel it in order to protect ourselves. Some child sexual assault survivors have forgotten how to respond to fear because they live with it constantly. This means a childhood where you can never relax, never trust and never be spontaneous, or a childhood where you take risks constantly because nothing worse can happen or you want to die, or because taking risks make you feel alive.

Adult survivors can have fears of never recovering, fears about sexuality, fear of feeling, fear of being a perpetrator, being weak, being powerless, being assaulted again, fear of being close to someone, fear of being a parent, fear of failure or fear of success.

Men readily become involved in activities which protect themselves from feeling fear. Fear is seen as such an 'anti-male' emotion. Throughout history men are supposed to be ready and able to defend themselves and others and this stereotype is confirmed throughout society. Women are equally conditioned to believe men are in control, fearless, brave, never vulnerable and always able to protect. Fears become stronger and more intense when they are hidden and it can help you break free to admit them. After all, most people are scared of something.

> *I've always been scared of the dark because the bad things happened in the dark. I still keep the hall light on at night but now the kids have left home I don't have an excuse any more, but I have to do it otherwise I'd stay awake all night waiting for him just as I did as a boy.*

> *I find it really difficult to be alone with another man. I'm frightened he may be sexual with me and I'd just freak. I can't go to a male doctor or anything.*

Loneliness

Most survivors struggle with loneliness and feelings of isolation. This is usually about feeling different and damaged. There is a need to hide your real self or you will be rejected if people knew what had happened to you. Survivors can develop a fear of intimacy because of this and an inability to trust themselves or others. Some people avoid close relationships to protect themselves. Avoiding close relationships mirrors the essential isolation of the child when he was assaulted and was isolated by shame, fear and secrecy.

Survivors often have difficulty making the connections with other people which would reduce their feelings of isolation. It is partly because it is so hard to trust others after the experience of sexual trauma and it is so hard to trust yourself. Recovery usually involves taking a risk in relationships and accepting that you can be accepted and loved for who you are. A counselling relationship can be the starting point for re-establishing some trust and many survivors find the intimacy of counselling very difficult at first.

> *I eventually told my mother when I was twenty about what had happened when I was 12 with the neighbour's son. Although she was so upset I felt a huge relief because everything made sense to her. I know she was upset that I had not been able to tell her before and she felt really guilty. I realised then how I'd deprived myself of her support for all those years. After that, I found I could tell other people and I didn't feel so ashamed.*

Sexuality

It stands to reason that men who have experienced sexual assault either as a child or an adult will find that it has an impact on how they express themselves sexually. This is partly because sex and sexual assault become confused as the same thing (when they are not) but also because men are taught that sexuality is an acceptable way to be emotional. Adult survivors may find that consensual sex and intimacy intensifies the emotions which the assaults created.

Sexuality is something we are all born with and is meant to be initially discovered and explored alone, at one's own pace and in one's own way. It progresses naturally then to being shared with others. Child sexual assault interrupts that part of development and takes a child's sexuality out of their control. Child sexual assault will sexualise a child before they have the mental ability to understand what is happening. Sexuality can become intrinsically linked with the assault experience.

Survivors may find that sexual activity makes them feel guilty, vulnerable, ashamed, afraid, dirty, disgusted. It may create feelings of emptiness and loneliness. There may be physical and emotional arousal to pain, humiliation or coercion. Survivors may have fantasies about the assaults which make them feel re-abused. There may be flashbacks or other re-experiencing of the assaults. Survivors may feel their only value is as a sexual being and define all physical contact in sexual ways. There may be extreme anxiety about sexual performance.

These feelings may result in a number of sexual difficulties; difficulty achieving or maintaining an erection, premature ejaculation, difficulty ejaculating, compulsive masturbation, fetishes, avoiding a sexual act. Male survivors can respond to their sexuality in various ways. Some will avoid all sexual contact with others, some will seek sexual activity constantly, others may 'go through the motions' but never let themselves feel closeness or intimacy with others, others may place themselves continuously in abusive situations.

In addition to survivors' struggles with their individual experiences they also have to cope with society's views about male survivors being 'weak', 'gay' or 'abusive'. This makes it so much harder to disclose and seek support when you believe that you may be labelled this way. These stereotypes must be challenged as they are based on fear and lack of knowledge. Society tends to demonise what it does not understand. It is worth looking at the facts.

No one is sure how sexual orientation develops but we do know that, in all cultures, 10 per cent of the population is sexually orientated to their own gender, regardless of whether those people have been sexually abused or not (Lew, 1988). There are gay and straight survivors and it does not appear that child sexual abuse *causes* sexual orientation or that child sexual abuse *happens* because of sexual orientation. What does happen is that child sexual abuse creates fear and confusion for the survivor about sexual orientation but it does not determine sexual orientation. For the survivor who is gay, or thinks he may be, there is added trauma in dealing with a homophobic world which results in additional stress.

The widely held idea that male survivors become child abusers forces men to keep silent. It is a myth that achieves credibility because it makes a nice and easy explanation for child sexual assault. While some perpetrators have a history of child sexual assault, many do not, although they are likely to have a history of childhood abuse of other kinds. Most male survivors do not become abusers although this is what they fear and they can become hypersensitive to any contact with children. This can make survivors punish themselves again by avoiding 'normal' contact with other people. If you do believe you are at risk of assaulting children it is important to seek some help. There are skilled professionals who work with offending behaviour who can help you deal with the problem. Most work with offenders will address the victim issues as well.

The view that male survivors are weak is linked to the whole way men and women are seen in our society. Women are frequently believed to be 'lesser' human beings in a range of ways and when men are seen as 'weak' they are categorised with women. It is a deeply sexist view which demeans both men and women. The rigid characteristics that men and women are expected to have is damaging to each individual's right to develop as people.

Sexist ideas are a trap which needs to be resisted by the survivor because far from being weak, child sexual assault survivors are immensely strong. After all, they have, all alone, survived extreme trauma.

> *I used to seek out sex wherever I could and if I couldn't find a partner, I'd masturbate, sometimes 15 or 20 times a day. But I always felt so bad afterwards. Eventually, my counsellor suggested that I was seeking something other than sexual satisfaction. I realised that what I wanted was an emotional satisfaction.*

> *For years I thought that what had aroused my perpetrator aroused me too. As I began to recover I became aroused by different things and I began to discover my own sexuality.*

> *When I was with a partner I just could not ejaculate, I couldn't lose control. It took a long time before I could make the connection with the abuse.*

Chapter 5

PRACTICAL HELP

Police/Legal

The legal system has many flaws when it deals with sexual assault. It is based on the law not on fairness. It is, however, the only system we have and for many people trying to get some form of justice, it is vital for their recovery. Sexual assault is a serious crime and making a report to the police can be a major step in acknowledging that wrong was done to you. It is now accepted that many victims of childhood sexual assault may wait years before they report and many prosecutions take place years after the crimes were committed. If you believe that reporting the assaults will be helpful for your recovery do not let the fact that it happened a long time ago deter you.

It is a good idea to have some understanding of the police/legal process as it can be long and harrowing and best started with some knowledge of what to expect.

If you have been recently raped or sexually assaulted it is important to inform the police as soon as possible so that they can collect physical evidence from your body and the crime scene.

Often prosecutions do not take place simply because the police know there is not enough evidence to succeed in the courts. This does not mean that you are not believed but that successful prosecutions are rare, mainly because it is a crime that takes place in secret and will involve one person's word against another.

It is worth remembering that only a fraction of cases of sexual assault go all the way through the legal process. The cases that do succeed tend to involve more than one victim, some kind of witness or other evidence that proves what happened. The other cases which succeed involve offenders who admit their guilt so there is no trial.

The first step is to report to the police. Making your statement can be long and painful but many people report some relief after doing it. The police require a lot of detail about the assault and the circumstances. It is reassuring to know that the police are becoming more aware of male sexual assault. You should not be subjected to comments on your sexuality, appearance, actions during the assault or any derogatory words or actions. If you are, you should consider making a complaint to the senior officer. Your statement is the main evidence a case is based on. If English is not your first language an interpreter should be made available for you. If the assault was recent, the police will arrange for a medical examination which will collect physical evidence.

After making a statement a senior officer makes a decision about whether to take the matter further. If the offender admits to the crimes he is charged and given a court date. If the police believe there is sufficient evidence but the offender says he is innocent he will be charged and given a court date. In some cases the police may request that the offender is held in custody which is decided by a magistrate. The case (known as a brief) is then passed to the Crown Prosecution Service (CPS) and it enters the legal system. The CPS will decide whether to continue the case. Again, this is a decision based on whether they can make a reasonable case to prosecute rather than a decision about whether you are believed.

The next stage is an initial hearing in a Magistrates Court (no jury), where a number of different things can happen depending on the circumstances. There can be a committal hearing where the evidence is examined to determine if it should go to the Crown Court, or the case can be transferred directly to the Crown Court.

At the Crown Court, if the defendant pleads not guilty, a jury is convened and all the evidence is presented. The victim gives evidence and is cross examined. If the jury finds the defendant not guilty he is acquitted. If he is found guilty, 'beyond reasonable doubt', there is usually an adjournment before a sentencing hearing. At this hearing the judge has to take into account the defendant's history and circumstances before he sentences.

This is only a brief sketch of the court process and it is wise to get more information if you are involved with a prosecution. The court process is very slow and there are always delays and long waits between each stage. The experience of giving evidence is traumatic and you can expect your account of what happened to be strongly tested by the defence. They will attempt to discredit you and your story and it can be a humiliating and distressing experience. Despite that, it can also be very empowering to have done everything you can. It is strongly recommended that you find external support if you are to pursue the legal options.

There are increasing numbers of cases in the courts involving boys and men and the legal system is becoming more aware of male sexual assault.

Victim support exists across the country and are staffed by trained volunteers who will support you when making a statement or going to court. You can make direct contact with them or you can be referred by the police. Volunteers may visit you at home or elsewhere. They are free and confidential. They also run a witness service to offer specific support at court for you and your family.

Other legal options

- It can be possible to take out a private prosecution or to sue the perpetrator for damages. The burden of proof in a non criminal action is different in that it relies on 'balance of probabilities' rather than 'beyond reasonable doubt'. You need to consult a solicitor if you are considering these options.

- If the perpetrator continues to pose a threat to you an injunction can be taken out.
- Victims of sexual assault can apply for criminal injuries compensation. This can be quite a difficult and drawn out procedure and there are some people who believe that sexual assault claims are 'made up' to get compensation. This is, of course irrelevant, and the sums awarded are really very low compared to the crime. However, it is a useful option to consider and it can be powerful to have the crime against you acknowledged.

Medical

It is really important to have a forensic medical examination after a recent sexual assault for your own well-being and peace of mind. Although it may feel embarrassing and humiliating there are some very good, sensitive doctors around who will understand your concerns. After a rape or sexual assault you may have sexual and non-sexual injuries and need to be screened for sexually transmitted diseases, including HIV. Sometimes the difficulty in seeking medical advice may be less than the worry you may have about your health. It can also be a positive step forward in caring about yourself. You can go to your GP, family planning clinic or a Brook Advisory Centre.

Many adult survivors of childhood sexual assault retain a view of their body as damaged especially when there has been penetration. Because children's understanding of their bodies can be limited, many survivors can grow up believing that their body, or its functioning, is abnormal as a result of the assaults. Again, it can be helpful to see a doctor. If you do not feel able to consult a doctor you can access medical information through a library or the Net. In general, it can be a good idea to learn more about how the male body works as many survivors may have learnt about their body through the assault and, as such, may have incorrect ideas about what is normal.

Counselling

Counselling has often been a difficult option for men because it is seen as a sign of weakness and that 'real' men don't need help. Men are discouraged in our society from being vulnerable or needing support. As male sexual assault becomes better understood, more and more counselling options are available for men.

Counselling can provide a safe and confidential space for you to discuss the things that trouble you most. It can be helpful to talk to someone neutral whose feelings you do not have to be responsible for. It can give you access to knowledge about male sexual assault that will help you make sense of what has happened to you. Talking about what happened to you can be the major step in challenging beliefs you have held about being silent about the assault.

You can go to a counsellor at a sexual abuse service or you can go to a private counsellor/psychologist. Local lists can be found in the telephone directory. Do not hesitate to ask if the counsellor has knowledge or expertise in male sexual assault. You can ask about different counselling styles and what you can expect in terms of cost and length of sessions.

Trust your instincts with a counsellor. It is okay, if you do not feel comfortable with one, to try another. You do have a choice. Consider if you would prefer male or female. You did not have choices when you were sexually assaulted but you do have choices about how, and with whom, you recover.

Groups

Attending a group for men is an option which is best done after you have received some individual counselling. For a lot of men this is the most powerful action they have taken. The advantage of a group is how liberating talking to other male survivors can be. The hardest aspect of going to a group is the first meeting but you need to remember that everyone is very nervous. What seems to be most valuable about a group is being able to talk honestly about your feelings without fear of ridicule because everyone else feels similar emotions. You learn from other men facing similar issues and it can be a huge relief to know you are not alone and you are not so different.

The Internet

The internet is a great source of information for survivors and can also offer the opportunity to communicate with other survivors with total anonymity. There are many different sites available and you can join a chat room where you can read other people's comments and put your own. The information on the internet is mainly American but UK sites are being developed. The internet appears to be a means of getting useful information but a *serious note of caution* is required. The internet has become a playground for paedophiles who take advantage of sites for survivors. Even subscribing to a news group for sexual assault recovery can result in large amounts of exploitative pornography appearing on e-mail. Be very careful.

Books

There are a number of books available that deal with male sexual assault and these are listed in the Resources section. Some of them are written for workers in the field, others for survivors. The literature, in general, is American, with little local material. Despite that, there is a lot of useful information to be found which is usually available in libraries. You can also order books over the phone or the internet if you feel uncomfortable about buying books directly.

It can be painful to read about sexual assault but it can also give you the advantage of knowledge and a real sense that you are not alone.

Other Helpful Activities

Writing a journal or letters (not necessarily to send) to express how you feel can be helpful. Writing poetry, drawing, painting or creative work of any kind can help you move your emotions from inside you to something concrete. The important thing is to link the activity with how you feel and ensure that you do not hurt yourself and others in your process of resolving your experiences.

Survivors sometimes have a need to confront the perpetrator. This is best done after you have worked through some of your strongest feelings. Most people, when they see the abuser, feel the same as they did when it happened. It is best to confront only when you feel you are prepared for any outcome. Perpetrators are unlikely to admit their crimes and beg your forgiveness. They are far more likely to deny everything and blame you, suggesting you are mad or bad.

Sharing your experiences with others can be a powerful way of resolving things. You can choose to talk to someone neutral whose own feelings you do not have to cope with. You can choose to talk to people who care about you. Remember that you are not responsible for how other people react, you are only responsible for your own reactions.

The Tasks of Recovery

Recovering from sexual assault is a very personal journey. Some men choose outside support, others go it alone. Whichever way you choose, trust yourself to know what will help the most. Generally, the tasks of recovering are:

- Accepting that you were sexually assaulted.
- Putting full responsibility for the assault with the person who did it, not yourself.
- Safely experiencing and expressing the feelings you had at the time and the feelings you have now.
- Recognising how sexual assault has affected you, what you have lost, what you may have gained, how your relationships are influenced by it, and how it has affected how you see yourself.

- Forgiving yourself for being vulnerable.
- Realising you do not have to be alone and that you can find support.
- Recognising how strong you are. Remember that when you were assaulted you were alone and vulnerable. It takes immense personal courage to survive sexual trauma. Strength can be defined in many other ways than traditional male ways. You survived the assaults, you can survive your recovery.
- Breaking your secrecy and sharing the burden.
- Deciding on whether you need to do anything e.g. legal action, talking to family members, disclosing to others.
- Trusting yourself to recover in ways that are best for you.
- Reclaiming yourself, your sexuality, your life.
- Putting sexual assault in its place. What happened to you does not need to define you and it does not need to rule your life. You can move on.
- Take care of yourself. You deserve to love and be loved, to have fun and laughter in your life.

Information for Partners and Supporters

Supporters (or pro survivors) are words used to describe anyone who supports and cares for someone who has experienced sexual assault. They can include partners, friends, parents, siblings and colleagues. This section has been written to provide some brief guidelines for supporters and to recognise the value you have, and the difficulties you may encounter. Supporting someone you care about through the intensity of sexual assault recovery can be extremely stressful, painful, and often very rewarding.

The most useful thing you can do, for yourself, and the person you support, is to increase your knowledge about sexual assault. Information can assist by making you feel less helpless. It can help you make informed decisions about how best to support someone and give you a picture of what issues the survivor faces. There is a lot of good material around for partners in particular, which is listed in the Resources section.

It is also helpful to look at how the survivor's struggles affect you personally. Identifying exactly how the survivor's trauma impacts on you can give you some sense of control over how it makes you feel. This is particularly important for parents and siblings who knew the survivor during the assault experiences.

Relationships reflect how we all feel about ourselves and most of us play out childhood issues in our adult relationships. Recognising that aspects of a relationship may have more to do with past experiences than present reality can help to change things.

The most difficult aspects of recovery a survivor has to face are inevitably going to affect their relationships. Learning to trust, to overcome self-hatred, to reclaim sexuality, will all have dramatic effects on relationships. Intense feelings of anger, grief and shame will be expressed within close relationships.

Sometimes survivors will take their feelings out on the people closest to them. This can be distressing for you. You need to remind yourself that however much pain someone is in, they are still responsible for their actions. You never deserve to be hurt or abused.

As a supporter you need to look after yourself while you support someone else. Try and work out how you are affected and to identify your own feelings. What you feel is valid too. You may struggle with guilt, grief, revulsion, anger or feeling powerless. The survivor's experiences may revive your own issues about sexual assault or other trauma and you deserve your own supports for this. There are some support groups for parents and partners, or you could start your own with help from local sources.

Some feelings you have, like extreme rage or need for revenge may cause immense pressure on the survivor. Although it may be helpful for the survivor to know that you are angry on their behalf, action is best left for the survivor to decide on.

You cannot heal for a survivor, or make them seek help. They were not in control of the abuse, they must be in control of the pace, and the nature, of their own recovery. You will need to be patient with yourself and the person you support. You are only human and, as such, not perfect.

The greatest gift to a survivor is to be believed, to be trusted and to be listened to. Above all, do not give up hope for yourself or the survivor. People can and do recover from sexual assault. It takes time, patience, love and trust.

RESOURCES

Bass, Ellyn and Davis (1988). *The Courage to Heal*. New York: Harper and Row.
This is an excellent book which explores all aspects of recovery. It has exercises and other ideas for resolving difficulties. Although it was initially written for women the latest edition is inclusive of male experiences.

Biddulph, S. (1994). *Manhood*. Sydney: Finch Publishing.
A general look at masculinity and men's issues.

Bly, R. (1990). *Iron John: A Book About Men*. USA: Addison-Wesley.

Conroy, P. (1987). *The Prince of Tides*. Bantam Books.
A novel about sexual assault.

Davis, L. (1991). *Allies in Healing*. New York: HarperCollins.
An excellent resource for partners.

Engel, B. (1991). *Partners in Recovery*. New York: Ballantine Books.
This book addresses all supporters of survivors.

Grubman-Black, S.D. (1990). *Broken Boys, Mending Men: Recovery from Childhood Sexual Abuse*. New York: Ballantine Books.
A self help book.

Hunter, M. (1990). *Abused Boys: The Neglected Victims of Sexual Abuse*. New York: Fawcett Columbine.
This book has a number of survivors stories as well as articles from therapists.

Out of the Shadows

King, N. (1995). *Speaking Our Truth.* New York: Harperperennial.

Lew, M. (1988). *Victims no Longer.* New York: HarperCollins.
The best resource written for men, a survivors manual. If you only read one book this is the one to get.

Marsden, J. (1998). *Secret Men's Business.* Australia: Pan Mcmillan.
A book aimed at adolescents about masculinity.

Maltz, W. (1991). *The Sexual Healing Journey.* New York: HarperCollins.
An excellent resource that addresses the sexual aspects of recovery.

Thomas, T. (1989). *Men Surviving Incest.* Walnut Creek, CA: Launch Press.
Individual accounts of recovery.

Tobin, R. (1999). *Alone and Forgotten. The Sexually Abused Man.* Creative Bound.

Zilbergeld, B. (1992). *The New Male Sexuality.* New York: Bantam Books.
A useful and informative book on male heterosexuality generally.

76

Organisations and Helplines

Two useful web sites for survivors which detail resources for men are:

Abuse Recovery UK. http://aruk.co.uk
Abuse Survivors UK. http://asuk.co.uk

Many of the helplines also have web sites now.

The national helplines will provide you with information about local resources and your local telephone directory will list organisations.

Support Lines

1 in 4
020 8697 2112
Support for survivors of abuse in London and South East but will offer telephone support to all areas.

Careline
020 8514 1177
For all adult survivors.

Childhood Abuse Advisory Service (CAAS)
01255 435000

Child Abuse Survivors Network
Mails out a counselling pack. Send a SAE to PO Box 1, London N1 7SN.

Childline
0800 1111
For all children.

Gay Switchboard UK
0207 837 7324
Are well experienced with male rape.

Lifeline
01262 674 505
For all survivors. Offers telephone counselling.

Independent Care after Incestuous Relationship and Rape (ICAIRR)
01799 530 520 Essex
Provides counselling in person or on the phone.

MASA
0141 402 8349 Glasgow
Supports adult male survivors and their families.

Reachout
0208 905 4501
Volunteers offer support to survivors of childhood abuse and their families.

Relate
See telephone directory for your local number.
Many branches run support groups for survivors, and counselling if abuse issues are affecting your relationship.

Survivors UK
020 7833 3737
Helpline for male survivors is open Tuesday 7 to 10 pm.
Work with male survivors and their partners. Offer support groups.
Web address is http://www.survivorsuk.co.uk

REFERENCES

Briere, J. (1989). *Therapy for Adults Molested as Children: Beyond Survival.* New York: Springer Publishing Company.

Briggs, F. (1995). *From Victim to Offender.* NSW, Australia: Allen and Unwin.

Briggs, F., and Hawkins Russell M.F. (1996). A Comparison of the Childhood Experiences of Convicted Male Child Molesters and Men who were Sexually Abused in Childhood and Claim to be Non-offenders. *Child Abuse and Neglect,* 20: 3.

Bruckner, D.F., and Johnson, P.E. (1987). Treatment for Adult Male Victims of Childhood Sexual Abuse. *Social Casework: The Journal of Contemporary Social Work,* February.

Cermak, P., and Molidor, C. (1996). Male Victims of Child Sexual Abuse. *Child and Adolescent Social Work Journal,* 13(5) October.

Crome, S., McCabe, M., and Ford, L. (1999). Male Rape Victims: Fact and Fiction. *Law Institute Journal,* January.

Crowder, A. (1995). *Opening the Door.* New York: Brunner/Mazel.

Donaldson, S. (1990). Rape of Males. Dynes and Wayne, R. (Eds.). *Encycyclopedia of Homosexuality.* New York: Garland Publications.

Donnelly, D., and Kenyon, S. (1996). 'Honey, We don't do Men.' *Journal of Interpersonal Violence,* 11(3) September.

Finkelhor, D. (1986). *A Sourcebook on Child Sexual Abuse.* Newbury Park, CA: Sage.

Frazier, P. (1993). A Comparative Study of Male and Female Rape Victims Seen at a Hospital-based Rape Crisis Program. *Journal of Interpersonal Violence,* 8(1) March.

Gil, E. (1988). *Treatment of Adult Survivors of Childhood Abuse.* Walnut Creek, CA: Launch Press.

Groth, N., and Wolbert-Burgess, A. (1980). Male Rape: Offenders and Victims. *American Journal of Psychiatry,* 137.

Heilpern, D. (1997). *Fear or Favour: Sexual Assault of Young Male Prisoners.* Southern Cross University Press.

Hunter, M. (Ed.) (1990). *The Sexually Abused Male (Vols. 1 and 2).* New York: Lexington Books.

Mathews, F. (1996). *The Invisible Boy.* Canada: Family Violence Prevention.

O'Connor, C., and Petrakis, V. (1999). *Rockspider: The Danger of Paedophiles.* Melbourne: Hybrid.

Urquiza, A., and Capra, M. (1990). The Impact of Sexual Abuse: Initial and Long-term Effects. In Hunter, M. (Ed.). *The Sexually Abused Male (Vol. 1).* Lexington, MA: Lexington Books.

Watkins, W., and Bentovim, A. (1992). The Sexual Abuse of Male Children and Adolescents: A Review of Current Research. *Journal of Child Psychology and Psychiatry,* 33: 1.

Zilbergeld, B. (1992). *The New Male Sexuality.* New York: Bantam Books.